D1083761

TEAM SPIRIT®

SMART BOOKS FOR YOUNG FANS

THE ST. LOUIS RAMS

BY
MARK STEWART

NORWOODHOUSE PRESS

CHICAGO, ILLINOIS

Norwood House Press
P.O. Box 316598
Chicago, Illinois 60631

For information regarding Norwood House Press, please visit our website at:
www.norwoodhousepress.com or call 866-565-2900.

All photos courtesy of Getty Images except the following:
Icon SMI (4, 14), National Football League (6), Bowman Gum Co. (7, 17, 21), Hostess Brands (9),
Black Book Partners (11, 37, 39), Topps, Inc. (15, 20, 23, 28, 29, 30, 35 top left & right, 41, 42 both, 45),
St. Louis Rams (33), Author's Collection (34 left, 38, 43 bottom), Philadelphia Gum Co. (34 right),
Los Angeles Rams/NFL (36, 43 top), Xerographics, Inc. (40), Matt Richman (48).
Cover Photo: Icon SMI

The memorabilia and artifacts pictured in this book are presented for educational and informational purposes,
and come from the collection of the author.

Editor: Mike Kennedy
Designer: Ron Jaffe
Project Management: Black Book Partners, LLC.
Special thanks to Topps, Inc.

Library of Congress Cataloging-in-Publication Data

Stewart, Mark, 1960-
  The St. Louis Rams / by Mark Stewart.
     p. cm. -- (Team spirit)
  Includes bibliographical references and index.
  Summary: "A revised Team Spirit Football edition featuring the St. Louis
Rams that chronicles the history and accomplishments of the team. Includes
access to the Team Spirit website which provides additional information and
photos"--Provided by publisher.
  ISBN 978-1-59953-540-1 (library edition : alk. paper) -- ISBN
978-1-60357-482-2 (ebook) 1. St. Louis Rams (Football
team)--History--Juvenile literature. I. Title.
  GV956.S85S84 2012
  796.332'640977866--dc23
                                                    2012019096

Manufactured in the United States of America in North Mankato, Minnesota.
205N—082012

COVER PHOTO: The Rams celebrate a touchdown during the 2011 season.

Table of Contents

ABOUT OUR GLOSSARY

In this book, there may be several words that you are reading for the first time. Some are sports words, some are new vocabulary words, and some are familiar words that are used in an unusual way. All of these words are defined on page 46. Throughout the book, sports words appear in **bold type**. Regular vocabulary words appear in ***bold italic type***.

Meet the Rams

Teams in the **National Football League (NFL)** do a lot of traveling during a season. They play half their schedule in other cities and sometimes have to fly thousands of miles between games. The St. Louis Rams may be the most well-traveled team of all. During their history, they have moved twice.

No matter which city they've called home, the Rams have always put points on the scoreboard. Some of football's great passers, runners, and receivers have worn the team's blue and gold uniform. When it comes to stopping opponents from scoring, the Rams are pretty good, too.

This book tells the story of the Rams. In the rough and sweaty world of *professional* football, it isn't easy to be glamorous. Yet, somehow, the Rams always find a way to look like champions. They are spectacular in victory and courageous in defeat. Every player on the team gives his all to measure up to a long *tradition* of excellence.

Sam Bradford flicks a short pass to Lance Kendricks. The Rams have been famous for their passing game since the 1940s.

Glory Days

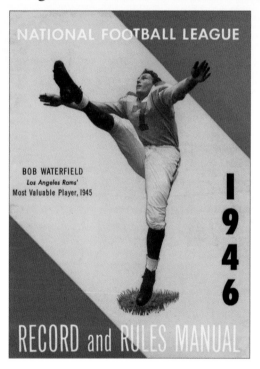

NATIONAL FOOTBALL LEAGUE

BOB WATERFIELD
Los Angeles Rams'
Most Valuable Player, 1945

1946

RECORD and RULES MANUAL

The state of Ohio has a proud football history. In fact, many people consider it to be the birthplace of the professional game. When the NFL announced plans to expand in 1937, the league turned to Cleveland, Ohio. The city already had a team called the Rams, and owner Homer Marshman was eager to be part of the NFL.

Cleveland's early stars included Johnny Drake, Chet Adams, Jim Benton, and Ted Livingston. They helped form a *competitive* team, but the Rams did not have a winning season until 1945. That year, a **rookie** named Bob Waterfield joined the club. He was a talented quarterback who also kicked **field goals**. The Rams found a perfect coach in Adam Walsh. He believed that strong-armed passers such as

Waterfield were the future of football. The Rams went 9–1 in 1945 and won their first NFL championship.

A few months later, fans were shocked to learn that the

PAUL "Tank" YOUNGER

Rams were moving to Los Angeles, California. Dan Reeves was now the team owner. He believed that the Rams would draw more fans out West, where the population was skyrocketing. Other sports teams had thought of doing the same thing. The Rams were the first to actually take the chance. It turned out to be a great move.

The Rams had a star-studded team. Waterfield and Norm Van Brocklin shared time at quarterback. Waterfield usually played the first and third quarters, and Van Brocklin would come in for the second and fourth quarters. They had two excellent receivers in Tom Fears and Elroy "Crazy Legs" Hirsch. Three big running backs—Dan Towler, Tank Younger, and Dick Hoerner—made up the "Bull Elephant" **backfield**.

Towler and Younger were two of the NFL's top African-American stars. In an *era* when there weren't many black players in the league, the Rams were pioneers. Other African-American stars who took the field for Los Angeles included Kenny Washington, Woody Strode,

LEFT: Bob Waterfield was picked to be on the cover of the NFL Guide in 1946.
ABOVE: Tank Younger was an early African-American star.

Dick "Night Train" Lane, and Bob Boyd. The team reached the **NFL Championship Game** four times from 1949 to 1955. The Rams won the league title once, in 1951.

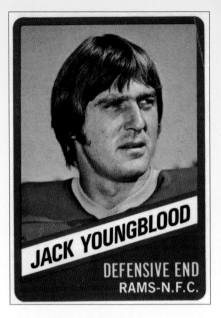

The team struggled after the glory years of the 1950s. By the mid-1960s, however, the Rams were competitive again. The key was their defensive line of Deacon Jones, Merlin Olsen, Rosey Grier, and Lamar Lundy—who together were known as the "Fearsome Foursome." They got help from linebackers Maxie Baughan and Jack Pardee and defensive backs Eddie Meador and Clancy Williams. Quarterback Roman Gabriel guided a strong offense that included receivers Jack Snow and Bernie Casey and running backs Les Josephson and Dick Bass.

Los Angeles won its **division** seven years in a row during the 1970s. The Rams reached the **Super Bowl** for the first time in 1980. Again, their defense led the way. Jack Youngblood, Jack Reynolds, Fred Dryer, and Isiah Robertson were all hard-hitting stars. The offense relied on a balanced attack that featured receiver Harold Jackson and running back Lawrence McCutcheon.

The Rams continued their fine play during the 1980s. Their best player was Eric Dickerson. He was a tall, graceful running back with

LEFT: Eric Dickerson
ABOVE: Jack Youngblood

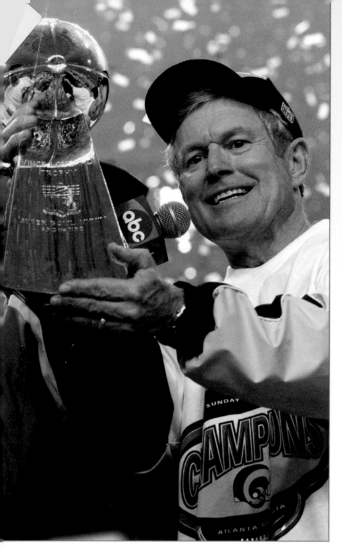

great speed and power. He was named the NFL Offensive Rookie of the Year in 1983 and rushed for more than 2,000 yards the following season. Always looking to improve, the team traded Dickerson in 1987 for a group of **draft choices**. After one losing season, Los Angeles returned to the **playoffs** two years in a row. In 1989, the team came within one victory of going to the Super Bowl.

In 1995, the Rams moved again, this time to St. Louis, Missouri. The Midwest city had once been home to the Cardinals, who now played in Arizona. The fans in St. Louis were hungry for another team of their own.

Under coach Dick Vermeil, the Rams won with a high-flying passing attack. Fans liked to call the St. Louis offense the "Greatest Show on Turf." Quarterback Kurt Warner had some of the NFL's best weapons, including running back Marshall Faulk and receivers Isaac Bruce and Torry Holt. No team in the NFL could match the Rams' firepower. In 1999, they took the championship of the **National Football Conference (NFC)** and then won Super Bowl XXXIV. It was the team's first title in almost 50 years.

Two seasons later, coach Mike Martz led the team back to the Super Bowl. Unfortunately, a field goal in the final seconds robbed the Rams of victory. In the years that followed, St. Louis continued to put exciting stars on the field, including Leonard Little, Adam Timmerman, Marc Bulger, Steven Jackson, and James Laurinaitis. However, as the team's *veterans* got older and retired, the Rams struggled to replace them.

In 2010, St. Louis decided to rebuild again. The Rams used the first pick in the draft to take Sam Bradford. The young quarterback showed talent and courage in his first season. He soon became a team leader. Two years later, the Rams hired Jeff Fisher as their coach. The fans in St. Louis were excited for the future. "The Greatest Show on Turf" was ready to make its return.

LEFT: Dick Vermeil shows off the Super Bowl trophy.
ABOVE: Kurt Warner warms up before a game.

Home Turf

For most of their time in Cleveland, the Rams played in a baseball stadium called League Park. After moving to California in 1946, they hosted their games in the Los Angeles Memorial Coliseum. In 1980, the team moved south to Anaheim Stadium, where it stayed through the 1994 season.

In St. Louis, the Rams had a beautiful domed stadium waiting for them. Fans love it because the seating design makes them feel like they can reach out and touch the players. In 2011, the team replaced the playing surface with a new *synthetic* turf. It is smooth and has good *traction*, which helps the Rams play their speedy style of football.

BY THE NUMBERS

- The Rams' stadium has 66,965 seats.
- The stadium cost $280 million to build and went through $30 million in improvements in 2009.
- The stadium's turf measures 73,000 square feet and weighs 100,000 pounds.

Matt Turk prepares to punt in the Rams' domed stadium.

Dressed for Success

The Rams have used many different colors and uniforms over the years. In Cleveland, they wore red and black. In 1938, the team switched to yellow and blue. Ten years later, running back Fred Gehrke painted yellow rams' horns on his blue helmet. Before long, the whole team followed his lead. It was the first time an NFL team featured a *logo* on its helmet.

In 1964, the Rams replaced the yellow in their uniforms with white. In 1973, they went back to yellow. Several years after moving to St. Louis, the team changed the yellow to a metallic gold. A logo of a ram's head was also added to the uniform.

In 2007, the team had a little fun with its uniform. The players wore every possible combination of tops and bottoms during the season. Fans had trouble keeping up with every uniform style!

LEFT: Steven Jackson wears the team's metallic gold pants.
RIGHT: Dan Towler's 1956 trading card shows the famous rams-horn helmet design.

We Won!

Some NFL teams have never won a championship. However, the Rams have claimed titles in three different cities. The first came in Cleveland in 1945. Rookie Bob Waterfield made a big splash that season. He topped all NFL quarterbacks with 14 touchdown passes, had six **interceptions** as a defensive back, and also served as the team's punter and kicker. His best receiver was Jim Benton. Fred Gehrke, Jim Gillette, and Don Greenwood were all talented running backs.

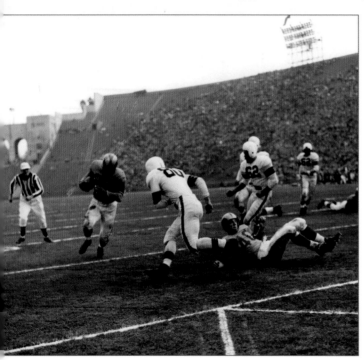

The Rams faced the Washington Redskins for the 1945 NFL championship on a windy day in Cleveland. They came alive in the second quarter when Waterfield threw a long touchdown pass to Benton. He tossed

LEFT: Dan Towler heads for the goal line against the Cleveland Browns in the 1951 title game.
RIGHT: Tom Fears

another in the third quarter, this time to Gillette. From there, the Rams tightened their defense and won 15–14.

The team's next championship came in 1951, after the Rams had moved to Los Angeles. Waterfield combined with Norm Van Brocklin to give the team a great passing attack. Together, they threw for 26 touchdowns in 12 games. Seventeen of those scoring tosses went to Elroy Hirsch. Dan Towler, Tank Younger, and Dick Hoerner handled the rushing duties.

In the NFL Championship Game, the Rams met the team that had replaced them in Cleveland, the Browns. They knew each other very well. One year earlier, the Browns had beaten the Rams for the title on a last-second field goal. This time, Los Angeles made the big play. With the score tied late in the contest, Van Brocklin launched a long pass to Tom Fears. He cradled the ball and raced into the end zone for a 73-yard touchdown. The Rams held on for a 24–17 victory.

It was nearly five *decades* before the Rams flew their next championship banner. By then, the team had moved to St. Louis. In 1999, the Rams had the game's most exciting offense. Quarterback Kurt Warner led the league with 41 touchdown passes and was named NFL **Most Valuable Player (MVP)**. Running back Marshall Faulk gained 1,381 yards on the ground and caught 87 passes for another 1,048 yards. Receivers Isaac Bruce and Torry Holt combined for 18 touchdowns.

In the playoffs, the Rams destroyed the Minnesota Vikings to advance to the **NFC Championship Game**. In a tense battle with the Tampa Bay Buccaneers, the St. Louis defense stepped up. The Rams had five **sacks** and two interceptions in an 11–6 victory.

That set up a meeting with the Tennessee Titans in Super Bowl XXXIV. The Rams raced to a 16–0 lead and looked like they were in complete control. However, the Titans tied the score with two

minutes left. Warner and Bruce came to the rescue. The pair hooked up on a 73-yard touchdown pass with time running out. The Titans had one last chance, but the St. Louis defense managed to stop them just short of the goal line. The Rams won 23–16 for the third championship in team history.

LEFT: Marshall Faulk scores against the Tampa Bay Buccaneers in the playoffs.
ABOVE: Isaac Bruce spins away from a tackler on the way to his game-winning score in Super Bowl XXXIV.

Go-To Guys

T o be a true star in the NFL, you need more than fast feet and a big body. You have to be a "go-to guy"—someone the coach wants on the field at the end of a big game. Rams fans have had a lot to cheer about over the years, including these great stars …

THE PIONEERS

BOB WATERFIELD   Quarterback/Kicker

• BORN: 7/26/1920   • DIED: 3/25/1983   • PLAYED FOR TEAM: 1945 TO 1952

Bob Waterfield was the finest all-around player of his time. He was the NFL passing champion twice and the league's top field-goal kicker three times. Waterfield often punted the ball more than 60 yards, and he also intercepted 20 passes during his career.

NORM VAN BROCKLIN   Quarterback

• BORN: 3/15/1926   • DIED: 5/2/1983

• PLAYED FOR TEAM: 1949 TO 1957

Norm Van Brocklin had a strong arm and a great desire to win. He always demanded the best from his teammates. Van Brocklin was voted into the **Hall of Fame** in 1971.

ELROY HIRSCH   Receiver

- BORN: 6/17/1923   • DIED: 1/28/2004   • PLAYED FOR TEAM: 1949 TO 1957

Elroy Hirsch was nicknamed "Crazy Legs" for his wild running style. In 1951, he had one of the greatest seasons in history. Hirsch led the NFL with 66 catches, 1,495 yards, and 17 touchdowns.

LES RICHTER   Linebacker/Kicker

- BORN: 10/26/1930   • DIED: 6/12/2010
- PLAYED FOR TEAM: 1954 TO 1962

The Rams made headlines in the 1950s when they traded 11 players to get Les Richter. He was a great tackler, blocker, and kicker. With the Rams, Richter played in the **Pro Bowl** eight years in a row.

MERLIN OLSEN   Defensive Lineman

- BORN: 9/15/1940   • PLAYED FOR TEAM: 1962 TO 1976

Merlin Olsen teamed up with Deacon Jones for 10 seasons on the defensive line. The two were an almost unstoppable pair. Olsen was named **All-Pro** 10 times and made the Pro Bowl in each of his first 14 seasons.

LAWRENCE McCUTCHEON   Running Back

- BORN: 6/2/1950   • PLAYED FOR TEAM: 1972 TO 1979

Lawrence McCutcheon ran for more than 1,000 yards four times from 1973 to 1977. In 1975, he became the first NFL player to rush for over 200 yards in a playoff game. In his last game as a Ram, Super Bowl XIV, he threw a touchdown pass.

LEFT: Norm Van Brocklin   **ABOVE**: Les Richter

ERIC DICKERSON   Running Back

- BORN: 9/2/1960   • PLAYED FOR TEAM: 1983 TO 1987

Eric Dickerson's size, speed, and toughness made him a nightmare for opposing defenses. He could power through defensive linemen and outrun defensive backs. In his first four seasons with the Rams, he gained nearly 7,000 yards and scored 57 touchdowns.

ISAAC BRUCE   Receiver

- BORN: 11/10/1972   • PLAYED FOR TEAM: 1994 TO 2007

Isaac Bruce teamed up with Torry Holt to give the Rams a great receiving duo. He had an amazing ability to change his speed and direction. Bruce caught 119 passes in 1995 and scored the touchdown that won Super Bowl XXXIV for the Rams.

KURT WARNER   Quarterback

- BORN: 6/22/1971   • PLAYED FOR TEAM: 1998 TO 2003

Kurt Warner developed a lightning-quick throwing style while playing in the **Arena Football League**. In the NFL, he was the league's top passer three years in a row. Warner was NFL MVP in 1999 and 2001.

MARSHALL FAULK   Running Back

- BORN: 2/26/1973   • PLAYED FOR TEAM: 1999 TO 2005

Marshall Faulk was the most dangerous running back in the NFL when he played for the Rams. Every time Faulk took a handoff or caught a pass, he was a threat to go all the way. In 2000 and 2001, he scored a total of 47 touchdowns.

TORRY HOLT   Receiver

• BORN: 6/5/1976   • PLAYED FOR TEAM: 1999 TO 2008

Torry Holt had breathtaking speed. He needed just the smallest opening in the defense to break free for a long gain. His best season came in 2003 when he had 117 receptions for 1,696 yards and 12 touchdowns. Holt finished behind Isaac Bruce as the team's all-time leading receiver.

STEVEN JACKSON   Running Back

• BORN: 7/22/1983   • FIRST YEAR WITH TEAM: 2004

Steven Jackson watched and learned from Marshall Faulk. However, while Faulk glided down the field, Jackson ran more like a bulldozer. He topped 1,000 yards every season from 2005 to 2011 and was voted to the Pro Bowl three times.

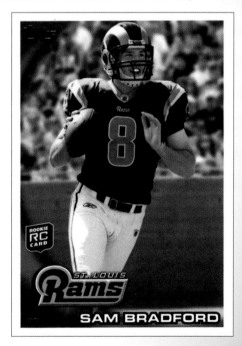

SAM BRADFORD   Quarterback

• BORN: 11/8/1987   • FIRST YEAR WITH TEAM: 2010

In 2010, the Rams made Sam Bradford the first pick in the draft. In his first eight games, he tied a record by throwing for 11 touchdowns. Bradford chose to wear jersey number 8 to honor Hall of Famer Troy Aikman. Aikman and Bradford both played in college for the University of Oklahoma.

RIGHT: Sam Bradford

Calling the Shots

The man calling the shots for the Rams' first championship was Adam Walsh. He coached the team during its last year in Cleveland and then its first year in Los Angeles. Walsh was a pioneer. He believed that the quarterback was the most important player on offense. Using the **T-formation**, Walsh turned the Rams into champions. Quarterback Bob Waterfield and receiver Jim Benton both became stars under Walsh.

The Rams continued to be a high-scoring team in the 1950s. Their coaches during this decade—Joe Stydahar, Hamp Pool, and Sid Gillman—loved the passing game. Stydahar and Pool both favored the long bomb. When they were in charge, the Rams could find the end zone from anywhere on the field. Under Gillman, the team experimented with short passes. He led the Rams to the NFL title game in his first season.

In the late 1960s, George Allen took over the Rams. For many years before that, he had run the defense for the Chicago Bears. Allen liked to create confusion and fear in opponents. He transformed the Rams into a defensive powerhouse. Chuck Knox

Kurt Warner and Dick Vermeil clap for team owner Georgia Frontiere during the Rams' Super Bowl celebration.

replaced Allen and won 54 games in just five seasons. Ray Malavasi had a similar record, leading the Rams to the playoffs eight years in a row. In 1980, he brought the team to the Super Bowl for the first time.

In 1997, team owner Georgia Frontiere hired Dick Vermeil as their coach. He teamed with assistant coach Mike Martz to give St. Louis a quick-strike offense that reminded many fans of the exciting Los Angeles teams of the 1950s. Vermeil led the Rams to victory in Super Bowl XXXIV in his third season. Martz took over as head coach and got the Rams back to the Super Bowl two years later.

One Great Day

Heading into the 1999 season, fans of the Rams believed their team was the best in the NFL—as long as Trent Green was their quarterback. When he got hurt in the preseason, they panicked. Fortunately, backup passer Kurt Warner kept his cool. He surprised everyone by throwing for more than 4,000 yards and 41 touchdowns. Warner led the league's best offense into Super Bowl XXXIV against the Tennessee Titans.

The Tennessee defense was every bit as good as the St. Louis offense. In the first quarter, Warner moved the Rams into scoring position, but St. Louis had to settle for a field goal. The Rams added two more short kicks to make it 9–0 at halftime. Early in the third quarter, Tennessee lined up for a field goal of its own. Todd Lyght blocked the kick to give the ball back to St. Louis. Warner marched the team down the field and flipped a short pass to Torry Holt in the end zone. The Rams led 16–0.

Mike Jones wraps up Kevin Dyson before he can stretch across the goal line.

The Titans fought back and tied the score at 16–16. The Rams got the ball with just over two minutes left in the game. Warner dropped back to pass and saw Isaac Bruce open. With the Titans pressuring him, Warner lofted a wobbly pass to Bruce. He caught the ball in stride and sprinted the rest of the way for a touchdown. The Rams led 23–16.

Again, the Titans fought back. They moved the ball to the St. Louis 10-yard line with enough time for one last play. Tennessee's Kevin Dyson caught a short pass and lunged for the goal line. Linebacker Mike Jones was waiting for him. He wrapped his arms around Dyson's legs and pulled him to the turf. Jones stopped Dyson just inches short of a touchdown.

The Rams were NFL champions for the first time since 1951. The difference between winning and losing came down to the final seconds and less than one yard. No Super Bowl had ever ended in such heart-stopping fashion.

Legend Has It

Deacon Jones

Was Deacon Jones the NFL's greatest pass-rusher?

LEGEND HAS IT that he was. Many people credit Jones with inventing the term "sack." His real name was David, but he nicknamed himself "Deacon" because it sounded cool. However, what people remember most about Jones is how good he was at blasting through the line and tackling the quarterback. In 1967 and 1968, Jones sacked the quarterback a total of 50 times—more than anyone in history over a two-year span. Unfortunately, sacks were not a statistic back then. Officially, Jones had zero sacks for those two seasons!

ABOVE: David "Deacon" Jones   RIGHT: This trading card shows the running style that earned Elroy Hirsch the nickname "Crazy Legs."

Which Rams legend could not outrun a group of kids?

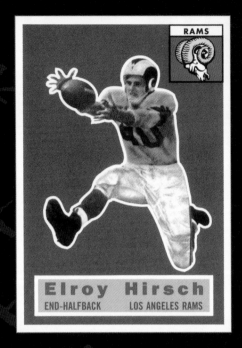

LEGEND HAS IT that Elroy Hirsch could not. In 1954, Hirsch announced that he would retire after the season. The Rams beat the Green Bay Packers in their last game, and Hirsch headed for the locker room. The only problem was that hundreds of young fans wanted souvenirs from their favorite player. They ran after Hirsch and began grabbing pieces of his uniform. By the time he escaped, he was wearing hip pads and ankle tape— and not much else! As it turned out, the fans would see more of Hirsch. He returned to the Rams for three more seasons.

Which Rams coach never had a driver's license?

LEGEND HAS IT that George Allen didn't. Allen spent almost every minute of the day thinking about football. He claimed that driving would distract him from what he loved the most. Instead of getting behind the wheel, Allen had someone drive him wherever he went.

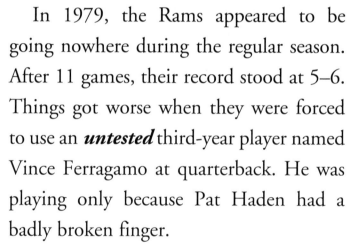

PAT HADEN

RAMS

QB

There is no bigger challenge in the NFL than reaching the Super Bowl. The Rams found this out during the 1970s. Season after season, they went to the playoffs, but they always fell short of the Super Bowl.

In 1979, the Rams appeared to be going nowhere during the regular season. After 11 games, their record stood at 5–6. Things got worse when they were forced to use an **untested** third-year player named Vince Ferragamo at quarterback. He was playing only because Pat Haden had a badly broken finger.

Most fans gave up on the season. Ferragamo had a different idea. This was his big chance—and he took advantage of it. With Ferragamo leading the way, the Rams won their next four games. Los Angeles finished 9–7 and won the **NFC West**.

Against the Dallas Cowboys in the playoffs, it looked like Ferragamo had run out of magic. In the first quarter, he was sacked in the end zone for a two-point safety. Again, Ferragamo didn't quit. He threw two touchdown passes in the second quarter and another with two minutes left in the game. The Rams won 21–19.

One week later, Ferragamo and the Rams faced the Tampa Bay Buccaneers in the NFC Championship Game. The winner would advance to the Super Bowl. Tampa Bay had the league's toughest defense, but Ferragamo was up to the challenge. On three different drives, he moved the Rams close enough to kick a field goal. That was all they needed for a 9–0 victory. For the first time in their history, the Rams reached the Super Bowl—and they owed it all to a backup quarterback!

Team Spirit

The Rams have played in three cities—and they've left their mark on all of them. In Cleveland, they were a beloved team. During almost five decades in Los Angeles, the Rams had the NFL's most glamorous fans. Dozens of television actors and movie stars could be found in the stands during home games.

During this era, many Rams were invited to appear on TV shows and in movies. Elroy Hirsch played himself in a movie called *Crazy Legs*. Bernie Casey and Rosey Grier became actors after their careers were over. In the 1980s, Merlin Olsen and Fred Dryer each starred in his own television series.

Since the team's move to St. Louis, the Rams have been treated like family. The fans celebrate every victory and support the team

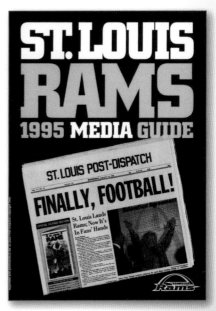

after losses. In return, the Rams make a great effort to get out and meet the fans. Few teams in football do as much for the community as the Rams do.

LEFT: Rams' fans have been known to take team spirit to extremes.
ABOVE: This guide is from the team's first year in St. Louis.

Timeline

In this timeline, each Super Bowl is listed under the year it was played. Remember that the Super Bowl is held early in the year and is actually part of the previous season. For example, Super Bowl XLVI was played on February 5, 2012, but it was the championship of the 2011 NFL season.

1952
Dick "Night Train" Lane has 14 interceptions as a rookie.

1945
The Rams win their first championship.

1937
The team joins the NFL as the Cleveland Rams.

1946
The Rams move to Los Angeles.

1969
Roman Gabriel is named NFL MVP.

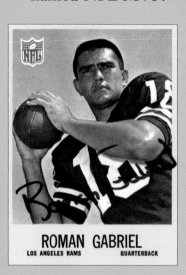

This program is from the team's days in Cleveland.

Roman Gabriel

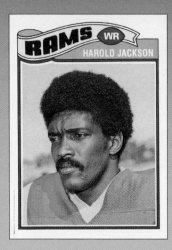

Harold
Jackson

Steven
Jackson

1973
Harold Jackson leads
the NFL with 13
touchdown catches.

1995
The Rams move
to St. Louis.

2006
Steven Jackson leads
the NFL with 2,334
total yards.

1989
Jim Everett leads the NFL
in touchdown passes for
the second year in a row.

2000
The Rams win Super
Bowl XXXIV.

2011
Chris Long has
13 sacks.

Isaac Bruce
celebrates a
Super Bowl
touchdown by
Torry Holt.

Fun Facts

CAPTAIN CRUNCH

Offensive linemen aren't usually considered team leaders in the NFL. Dennis Harrah was the exception. He served as the Rams' team captain for six seasons in the 1980s.

DOING HIS HOMEWORK

It was no fun trying to pass against the Rams in the late 1970s and early 1980s. That was because of Rod Perry, Pat Thomas, and Nolan Cromwell. Perry studied film of his opponents before each game. In 1978, his homework paid off when he returned three interceptions for touchdowns. Two years later, both Thomas and Cromwell were named All-Pro.

LONG TIME COMING

When the Rams drafted Sam Bradford in 2010, it was the first time since 1964 they used a first-round pick on a quarterback. That season, they selected Bill Munson.

ABOVE: Nolan Cromwell
RIGHT: Howie and Chris Long

LIKE FATHER, LIKE SON

The Rams drafted Chris Long with the second pick in the 2008 draft. He led the team in sacks in 2011. His father, Howie, was also a great pass-rusher. He was voted into the Hall of Fame in 2000.

WHAT ABOUT BOB?

Bob Waterfield may have been the NFL MVP in 1945, but he was still less famous than his wife. During his career with the Rams, he was married to superstar actress Jane Russell. In the 1950s, they formed a movie company together.

GEORGIA PEACH

In 1979, Rams owner Carroll Rosenbloom passed away. His wife, Georgia Frontiere, ran the team after that. During her 29 years as owner, the Rams went to the Super Bowl three times. In 1999, she became the first woman to own a Super Bowl championship team!

FEARS FACTOR

In 1949, Tom Fears set an NFL record with 77 catches. The following year, Fears broke his own record with 84 receptions—including 18 in one game!

Talking Football

"I don't think there's a defensive line to this day—or will be in the near future—that'll have that much balance."

► **Deacon Jones,** *on the "Fearsome Foursome"*

"Kurt Warner could handle more under pressure than any player I've ever been on the field with."

► **Dick Vermeil,** *on his star quarterback*

"The hardest part of the day for me was standing in that tunnel waiting for the game to get under way. I couldn't wait to get on the field."

► **Merlin Olsen,** *on the excitement he felt before games*

"My vision is my best *attribute*. I can see everything."
▶ **Marshall Faulk,** *on the key to his success as a running back*

"There are a lot of passes I want back. But it's not a yo-yo, it's a football."
▶ **Jim Everett,** *on throwing interceptions*

"As a competitor and someone who loves to play in big games, you've got to love going up against good teams."
▶ **Sam Bradford,** *on fighting for the NFC West crown every season*

"Put a football under Elroy's arm and he speeds up. Don't ask me how!"
▶ **Joe Stydahar,** *on Elroy "Crazy Legs" Hirsch*

LEFT: All four members of the Fearsome Foursome signed this photo.
ABOVE: Marshall Faulk

Great Debates

People who root for the Rams love to compare their favorite moments, teams, and players. Some debates have been going on for years! How would you settle these classic football arguments?

Nolan Cromwell was the team's greatest defensive back ...

... because he was a super-smart, super-tough safety who helped the Rams reach their first Super Bowl. In the early 1980s, no one at his position was better. In fact, he was voted the NFL's best defensive back four years in a row. Cromwell intercepted 37 passes in his career, and once he even substituted for the kicker and made an **extra point**!

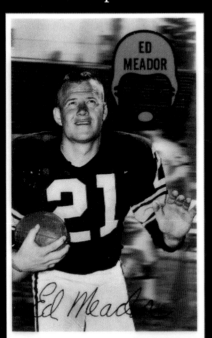

Eddie Meador wins this argument ...

... because he was a do-it-all star for the Rams in the 1960s. Meador (LEFT) blocked kicks, recovered **fumbles**, and intercepted passes. Quarterbacks worried just as much about him as they did about the famous Fearsome Foursome. Meador was an All-Pro six times and still holds the team record for interceptions with 46.

Bob Waterfield to Jim Benton was the best passing combination in team history ....

… because the pair turned the Rams into NFL champions. Benton had a talent for catching long passes. He had been on the team for several years before Waterfield arrived. The two clicked perfectly. In their first year together, Benton led the NFL in receiving yards, even though he played in just nine games. On Thanksgiving Day in 1945, he piled up 303 yards in receptions. That set a record that stood for more than 40 years!

Those guys were nothing compared to Kurt Warner and Isaac Bruce ....

… because that combination helped the Rams win their first Super Bowl. Bruce (RIGHT) was already one of the NFL's top receivers when Warner joined the team in 1998. The following season, the pair set the league on fire. From 1999 to 2001, Warner threw 98 touchdown passes, and 27 of those went to Bruce.

ISAAC BRUCE

For the Record

T he great Rams teams and players have left their marks on the record books. These are the "best of the best" …

Merlin Olsen

Isiah Robertson

RAMS AWARD WINNERS

WINNER	AWARD	YEAR
Parker Hall	Most Valuable Player	1939
Bob Waterfield	Most Valuable Player	1945
Dan Towler	Pro Bowl MVP	1952
George Allen	co-Coach of the Year	1967
Merlin Olsen	Pro Bowl Defensive MVP	1969
Roman Gabriel	Pro Bowl Offensive MVP	1969
Roman Gabriel	Most Valuable Player	1969
Isiah Robertson	Defensive Rookie of the Year	1971
Chuck Knox	Coach of the Year	1973
James Harris	Pro Bowl MVP	1975
Eric Dickerson	Offensive Rookie of the Year	1983
Eric Dickerson	Offensive Player of the Year	1986
Charles White	Comeback Player of the Year	1987
Greg Bell	Comeback Player of the Year	1988
Jerry Gray	Pro Bowl MVP	1990
Jerome Bettis	Offensive Rookie of the Year	1993
Dick Vermeil	Coach of the Year	1999
Marshall Faulk	Offensive Player of the Year	1999
Kurt Warner	Most Valuable Player	1999
Kurt Warner	Super Bowl XXXIV MVP	2000
Marshall Faulk	Offensive Player of the Year	2000
Marshall Faulk	Most Valuable Player	2000
Marshall Faulk	Offensive Player of the Year	2001
Kurt Warner	Most Valuable Player	2001
Mark Bulger	Pro Bowl MVP	2004
Sam Bradford	Offensive Rookie of the Year	2010

RAMS ACHIEVEMENTS

ACHIEVEMENT	YEAR
Western Division Champions	1945
NFL Champions	1945
Western Division Champions	1949
Western Division Champions	1950
Western Division Champions	1951
NFL Champions	1951
Western Conference Champions	1955
Coastal Division Champions	1967
Coastal Division Champions	1969
NFC West Champions	1973
NFC West Champions	1974
NFC West Champions	1975
NFC West Champions	1976
NFC West Champions	1977
NFC West Champions	1978
NFC West Champions	1979
NFC Champions	1979
NFC West Champions	1985
NFC West Champions	1999
NFC Champions	1999
Super Bowl XXXIV Champions	1999*
NFC West Champions	2001
NFC Champions	2001
NFC West Champions	2003

Super Bowls are played early the following year, but the game is counted as the championship of this season.

ABOVE: Carroll Rosenbloom owned the Rams from 1972 to 1979.
BELOW: This pennant celebrates the team's 2003 division championship.

Pinpoints

T he history of a football team is made up of many smaller stories. These stories take place all over the map—not just in the city a team calls "home." Match the pushpins on these maps to the **Team Facts**, and you will begin to see the story of the Rams unfold!

TEAM FACTS

1. St. Louis, Missouri—*The team has played here since 1995.*
2. Burlington, Iowa—*Kurt Warner was born here.*
3. Greensboro, North Carolina—*Torry Holt was born here.*
4. Cleveland, Ohio—*The team played here from 1937 to 1945.*
5. Minneapolis, Minnesota—*James Laurinaitis was born here.*
6. Elmira, New York—*Bob Waterfield was born here.*
7. New Orleans, Louisiana—*Isiah Robertson was born here.*
8. Atlanta, Georgia—*The Rams won Super Bowl XXXIV here.*
9. Oklahoma City, Oklahoma—*Sam Bradford was born here.*
10. Logan, Utah—*Merlin Olsen was born here.*
11. Los Angeles, California—*The team played here from 1946 to 1994.*
12. Guadalajara, Mexico—*Tom Fears was born here.*

James Laurinaitis

Glossary

🧠 **Football Words**
🧠 **Vocabulary Words**

🧠 **ALL-PRO**—An honor given to the best players at their positions at the end of each season.

🧠 **ARENA FOOTBALL LEAGUE**—An indoor football league that began play in 1987.

🧠 *ATTRIBUTE*—A personal quality.

🧠 **BACKFIELD**—The players who line up behind the line of scrimmage. On offense, the quarterback and running backs are in the backfield.

🧠 *COMPETITIVE*—Having a strong desire to win.

🧠 *DECADES*—Periods of 10 years; also specific periods, such as the 1950s.

🧠 **DIVISION**—A group of teams that play in the same part of the country.

🧠 **DRAFT CHOICES**—College players selected or "drafted" by NFL teams each spring.

🧠 *ERA*—A period of time in history.

🧠 **EXTRA POINT**—A kick worth one point, attempted after a touchdown.

🧠 **FIELD GOALS**—Goals from the field, kicked over the crossbar and between the goal posts. A field goal is worth three points.

🧠 **FUMBLES**—Balls that are dropped by the players carrying them.

🧠 **HALL OF FAME**—The museum in Canton, Ohio, where football's greatest players are honored. A player voted into the Hall of Fame is sometimes called a "Hall of Famer."

🧠 **INTERCEPTIONS**—Passes that are caught by the defensive team.

🧠 *LOGO*—A symbol or design that represents a company or team.

🧠 **MOST VALUABLE PLAYER (MVP)**—The award given each year to the league's best player; also given to the best player in the Super Bowl and Pro Bowl.

🧠 **NATIONAL FOOTBALL CONFERENCE (NFC)**—One of two groups of teams that make up the NFL.

🧠 **NATIONAL FOOTBALL LEAGUE (NFL)**—The league that started in 1920 and is still operating today.

🧠 **NFC CHAMPIONSHIP GAME**—The game played to determine which NFC team will go to the Super Bowl.

🧠 **NFC WEST**—A division for teams that play in the western part of the country.

🧠 **NFL CHAMPIONSHIP GAME**—The game played to decide the winner of the league each year from 1933 to 1969.

🧠 **PLAYOFFS**—The games played after the regular season to determine which teams play in the Super Bowl.

🧠 **PRO BOWL**—The NFL's all-star game, played after the regular season.

🧠 *PROFESSIONAL*—Paid to play.

🧠 **ROOKIE**—A player in his first year.

🧠 **SACKS**—Tackles of the quarterback behind the line of scrimmage.

🧠 **SUPER BOWL**—The championship of the NFL, played between the winners of the National Football Conference and American Football Conference.

🧠 *SYNTHETIC*—Made in a laboratory, not in nature.

🧠 **T-FORMATION**—An offensive set in which three running backs line up in a row behind the quarterback to form a "T."

🧠 **TOTAL YARDS**—Rushing yards plus receiving yards.

🧠 *TRACTION*—A force that provides a surface with good footing.

🧠 *TRADITION*—A belief or custom that is handed down from generation to generation.

🧠 **UNTESTED**—Not yet proven.

🧠 *VETERANS*—Players with great experience.

OVERTIME

TEAM SPIRIT introduces a great way to stay up to date with your team! Visit our **OVERTIME** link and get connected to the latest and greatest updates. **OVERTIME** serves as a young reader's ticket to an exclusive web page—with more stories, fun facts, team records, and photos of the Rams. Content is updated during and after each season. The **OVERTIME** feature also enables readers to send comments and letters to the author! Log onto:

www.norwoodhousepress.com/library.aspx

and click on the tab: **TEAM SPIRIT** to access **OVERTIME**.

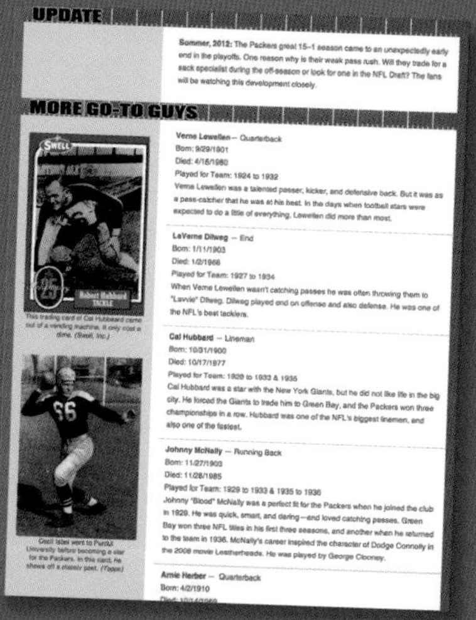

UPDATE

Summer, 2012: The Packers great 15–1 season came to an unexpectedly early end in the playoffs. One reason why is their weak pass rush. Will they trade for a sack specialist during the off-season or look for one in the NFL Draft? The fans will be watching this development closely.

MORE GO-TO GUYS

Verne Lewellen — Quarterback
Born: 9/29/1901
Died: 4/16/1980
Played for Team: 1924 to 1932
Verne Lewellen was a talented passer, kicker, and defensive back. But it was as a pass-catcher that he was at his best. In the days when football stars were expected to do a little of everything, Lewellen did more than most.

LaVerne Dilweg — End
Born: 1/11/1903
Died: 1/2/1968
Played for Team: 1927 to 1934
When Verne Lewellen wasn't catching passes he was often throwing them to "Lavvie" Dilweg. Dilweg played end on offense and also defense. He was one of the NFL's best tacklers.

Cal Hubbard — Lineman
Born: 10/31/1900
Died: 10/17/1977
Played for Team: 1929 to 1933 & 1935
Cal Hubbard was a star with the New York Giants, but he did not like life in the big city. He forced the Giants to trade him to Green Bay, and the Packers won three championships in a row. Hubbard was one of the NFL's biggest linemen, and also one of the fastest.

Johnny McNally — Running Back
Born: 11/27/1903
Died: 11/28/1985
Played for Team: 1929 to 1933 & 1935 to 1936
Johnny "Blood" McNally was a perfect fit for the Packers when he joined the club in 1929. He was quick, smart, and daring—and loved catching passes. Green Bay won three NFL titles in his first three seasons, and another when he returned to the team in 1936. McNally's career inspired the character of Dodge Connolly in the 2008 movie Leatherheads. He was played by George Clooney.

Arnie Herber — Quarterback
Born: 4/2/1910

Read all the books in the series to learn more about professional sports. For a complete listing of the baseball, basketball, football, and hockey teams in the **TEAM SPIRIT** series, visit our website at:

www.norwoodhousepress.com/library.aspx

On the Road

ST. LOUIS RAMS
701 Convention Plaza
St. Louis, Missouri 63101
314-982-7267
www.stlouisrams.com

THE PRO FOOTBALL HALL OF FAME
2121 George Halas Drive NW
Canton, Ohio 44708
330-456-8207
www.profootballhof.com

On the Bookshelf

To learn more about the sport of football, look for these books at your library or bookstore:

- Frederick, Shane. *The Best of Everything Football Book.* North Mankato, Minnesota: Capstone Press, 2011.
- Jacobs, Greg. *The Everything Kids' Football Book: The All-Time Greats, Legendary Teams, Today's Superstars—And Tips on Playing Like a Pro.* Avon, Massachusetts: Adams Media Corporation, 2010.
- Editors of *Sports Illustrated for Kids. 1st and 10: Top 10 Lists of Everything in Football.* New York, New York: Sports Illustrated Books, 2011.

Index

PAGE NUMBERS IN **BOLD** REFER TO ILLUSTRATIONS.

About the Author

MARK STEWART has written more than 50 books on football and over 150 sports books for kids. He grew up in New York City during the 1960s rooting for the Giants and Jets, and was lucky enough to meet players from both teams. Mark comes from a family of writers. His grandfather was Sunday Editor of *The New York Times,* and his mother was Articles Editor of *Ladies' Home Journal* and *McCall's.* Mark has profiled hundreds of athletes over the past 25 years. He has also written several books about his native New York and New Jersey, his home today. Mark is a graduate of Duke University, with a degree in history. He lives and works in a home overlooking Sandy Hook, New Jersey. You can contact Mark through the Norwood House Press website.